No More Pranks

Monique Polak

ORCA BOOK PUBLISHERS

Library and Archives Canada Cataloguing in Publication

Polak, Monique
No more pranks / Monique Polak.
(Orca soundings)

ISBN 10: 1-55143-584-5 (bound) / ISBN 10: 1-55143-315-x (pbk.)
ISBN 13: 978-1-55143-584-8 (bound) / ISBN 13: 978-1-55143-315-8 (pbk.)

I. Title. II. Series.
PS8631.O43N6 2004   JC813'.6   C2004-905171-7

First published in the United States, 2004
Library of Congress Control Number: 2004112466

Summary: Pete has to pull the most important prank of his life to bring about justice.

Mixed Sources
Cert no. SW-COC-001271
© 1996 FSC
FSC

Orca Book Publishers is dedicated to preserving the environment and has printed this book on paper certified by the Forest Stewardship Council.

Orca Book Publishers gratefully acknowledges the support for its publishing programs provided by the following agencies: the Government of Canada through the Canada Book Fund and the Canada Council for the Arts, and the Province of British Columbia through the BC Arts Council and the Book Publishing Tax Credit.

Cover design by Teresa Bubela
Cover photography by Eyewire

ORCA BOOK PUBLISHERS
PO BOX 5626, Stn. B
Victoria, BC Canada
V8R 6S4

ORCA BOOK PUBLISHERS
PO BOX 468
Custer, WA USA
98240-0468

www.orcabook.com
Printed and bound in Canada.

13 12 11 10 • 7 6 5 4

*For my Michael with love and gratitude
for bringing me to the whales.*

Chapter One

I'm not going to think about yesterday. No, I'm going to lie here under the covers and think about last week instead. Yesterday sucked big-time, but last week, well, last week was amazing.

One thing's for sure—I'm good. I don't mean good in a goody-goody way, like that girl Elizabeth who sits in the front row in English, the one who's always volunteering to erase the blackboard or run errands for the teacher. When I say I'm good, I mean I'm bad. Real bad.

It must've been pure badness that gave me the idea to phone the *Pillow Talk* hotline and pretend I was Mr. Quincy. That and the fact that he gave me a detention the week before for not having my shirt tucked in. You'd figure a vice-principal would have better things to do than patrol the hallways looking for dress-code violations. If you ask me, any self-respecting guy who goes around with a clear plastic ruler and measures the platforms on girls' shoes is asking for trouble.

Which is what I gave him.

When I got the idea, it was like I was possessed. Nothing could've stopped me—not even if I'd known how royally pissed off my parents would be.

Everyone at school listens to *Pillow Talk*. It's a total hoot. These perverts phone in to discuss their sexual problems. You'd think they'd be shy to talk about stuff like that on the radio, but they're not. Like this one nutbar phoned to say he likes to prance around naked right in front of his living-room window. He wanted to know if Dr. Dingle—believe it or not, that's the name of the sex therapist who hosts the show—thought there was anything wrong with that. Then there was this headcase who phoned to discuss her urge to tie her boyfriend up before they fooled around. You gotta admit, sometimes people can be pretty whacked out. It makes me wonder about regular-looking people I see in the street or at the mall. I want to ask them, Are you one of those weirdos or what?

I was pretty surprised when Dr. Dingle picked up the phone himself. I knew it was him because I would have recognized his voice anywhere. I *have* been listening to him twice a week since seventh grade. He's got one of those low, really serious voices and he says "uh-huh" and "I see" a lot. He also makes this clucking sound when people say how lousy they feel.

Which is exactly what he did with me. Only, it wasn't really me. It was me pretending to be Mr. Quincy. And I must have been convincing because Dr. Dingle fell for it—hook, line and sinker. "My name is Mr. Joseph Quincy," is how I started. My voice was a bit shaky at first. Not because I was nervous or anything, but because I was trying not to laugh. But even the shakiness was good, because most of the people who phone in sound nervous, especially when they first start talking. "I'm the vice-principal of Hill Road High School and I have a terrible problem."

I even sniffled a little to make myself sound extra pathetic.

That's when Dr. Dingle clucked. "And what is the nature of that problem?" he wanted to know.

"Well," I said—and I took a deep breath so I wouldn't crack up altogether—"I have an uncontrollable urge that involves girls' shoes. When I measure the platforms on their shoes, which is part of my job—you see, girls at Hill Road are forbidden to wear platforms more than two inches high—I'm unable to resist sniffing their shoes and feet. There's more, but it's extremely difficult for me to talk about on-air."

"Go ahead," Dr. Dingle prompted me, and then he made another of his clucking noises.

"Well," I continued, "I have this, this urge—it's really extremely shameful. I have an uncontrollable urge to brush

5

my private parts against these girls' stocking feet. Please, Dr. Dingle, help me!"

"Uh-huh, I see," and then Dr. Dingle took a short pause, as if he needed to gather his thoughts. "Well, the first thing you need to know, Joseph, is that foot fetishes are surprisingly common and relatively harmless," Dr. Dingle said. "But for a man in your, uh, position, it might be wise if you put someone else in charge of measuring footwear at your school. You are, shall we say— vulnerable. You don't mention a wife, Joseph, and I'm wondering whether you are married or have a girlfriend. Perhaps she might be willing to let you caress her feet. How does that sound, Joseph?"

That's when I slammed down the phone. I had to—because I was about to crack up.

My biggest mistake was taping the call. Okay, maybe it was my second biggest. The biggest was letting Jordan borrow the tape.

Everyone was whispering when I walked into homeroom on Monday. They were asking each other if they'd heard *Pillow Talk* the night before. Even Elizabeth was giggling. Then I remembered how, earlier in the year, she'd gotten into trouble for breaking the two-inch platform rule, so maybe even Elizabeth the goody-goody had something against Mr. Quincy.

"I'll bet it was you, right?" Jordan called out when I grabbed a seat near his. The other kids turned around to watch my reaction. I could have said it wasn't me, but I guess I was proud. I know it sounds kind of weird, but I felt like an artist or something. Like it was my creation and I wanted credit for it. I never could understand those guys who write poems and sign them "Anonymous." I mean, why go to all that trouble finding just the right words for what you're trying to say?

"Yup," I said, "it was me." And just for fun, I took a bow, bending over like I was on stage or something.

"Gee, am I ever sorry I missed it!" Jordan said. "We were out for dinner. But I heard all about it. 'An uncontrollable urge to brush your private parts...' Jeez, Larkin, how do you come up with that kind of stuff?" he said, clapping me on the shoulder.

I've known Jordan forever—which in our case is since we were both born—fifteen-and-a-half years ago. Our moms met in some prenatal yoga class. Unlike me (I'm just over five feet), Jordan's real tall. It's weird how much a guy's life is affected by his height. Jordan's into basketball. I've made a name for myself by pulling pranks.

"You can always listen to the tape," I told Jordan.

"You *taped* it?" Jordan sounded impressed.

"Uh-huh," I said, pulling the cassette out of my back pocket.

Jordan swears he had nothing to do with Mr. Quincy finding out, though he did admit he made two copies of the tape and lent them to some guys on the basketball team.

Mr. Quincy sure can't take a joke. When he called me into his office, his face looked like a purple balloon about to explode. "You have defamed my character. And I want you OUT OUT OUT!" I swear he said the word *out* three times. Not only am I suspended for five days, but I've actually got to switch high schools.

You can imagine how flipped out my parents are. Quincy met with them on Friday afternoon and my mom hasn't spoken to me since. Even my dad, who's usually pretty understanding when I get into trouble, is upset. "We're still reeling from all this," he told me yesterday when he passed me on the staircase at home. "This time, Pete, you've crossed the line."

No wonder I prefer to lie here and think of what last week was like. Before I crossed the line, that is.

My mom and dad don't argue much, but hey, they're arguing now. I can hear them all the way from the kitchen. They're making so much noise the floor in my bedroom is vibrating. "He's going—and that's that," my mom is saying.

Going where? What's going on?

"I've had it. He's spending the summer in Tadoussac. I want him away from those friends of his. And Daisy and Jean have offered to look after him."

Tadoussac? They've got to be kidding. That tourist trap in the middle of nowhere?

I can hear my dad's voice now. He'll talk her out of it. At least I hope he will.

"I'm not sure it's necessary," he says, "but if you think it's come to that..."

I can just imagine him throwing his arms up in the air.

Getting suspended is one thing. Being forced to go to another school is another. But spending a summer in Tadoussac? Now that's a life sentence.

Chapter Two

Pierre?

That's what everyone here calls me. And it doesn't help to say my name is Pete. They just nod and say, "Okay, Pierre." Then they point to the wet suits that need hosing down or the kayaks that have to be pushed off from the shore.

My Uncle Jean owns a kayaking company up here in Tadoussac, about five hours northeast of Montreal. He's got quite the job. Twice a day, he takes groups of tourists out on the St. Lawrence River to watch whales. You should see his tan.

Aunt Daisy—she's my mom's kid sister and Uncle Jean's wife—says the business is tougher than it looks. "Let's put it this way," she told me this morning at breakfast. "You don't want to be out on the river with a group of inexperienced kayakers when it's storming. If someone falls in, Jean has less than five minutes to get the person back in the kayak. The St. Lawrence might look harmless—just a body of gray-blue water—but it's colder than you'd expect. If you fall in, you lose sensation in your extremities—your hands and feet—within three minutes."

Aunt Daisy looks like my mom— they both have this wild, curly, blond hair—but they're not at all alike in other ways. My mom would definitely flip out if she were discussing losing sensation in your extremities. Not Aunt Daisy. You'd think she was discussing a recipe for sugar pie, this dessert she makes. Aunt Daisy is the calm, collected type. Maybe it's because she used to be a nurse. Up here though, she runs a bed-and-breakfast—the Whale's Tale—which is where she and Uncle Jean live—and where I'm staying.

It's funny about the St. Lawrence. I've spent my whole life in Montreal, and though the St. Lawrence is always there—underneath us when we cross one of the bridges into the city, or in the distance when we're up on Mount Royal—somehow, I never really noticed it till I got here. Man, that thing is massive. If you ask me, it's more like an ocean than a river.

Uncle Jean's got me working, which is all right, I guess. Otherwise,

I don't know what else I'd do up here in Dullsville. How many times can a guy go to the whale museum and check out whalebones? Of course I don't have Uncle Jean's cushy job out on a kayak. I'm part of the cleanup crew. But I get minimum wage, which means I should end up with about a thousand big ones by the end of August.

The other guys on the crew are older than me. Most of them don't speak much English, so it's a good thing I'm pretty much bilingual. As long as they don't talk too fast, I get most of what they say. I hate to admit it, but maybe all those years in French immersion schools weren't as big a waste as I thought.

One thing I notice is that I get all the crappy jobs. Like today, Réal— he's in charge when my uncle's not around—well, he made me hose down this mountain of boat shoes. They're these blue and silver nylon boots you're supposed to wear when you kayak. I guess they're meant to keep those extremities warm in case of a spill. You wouldn't believe how smelly those things get. I thought I'd pass out when I had a whiff of them.

Even though they didn't make a sound, I could tell that Réal and his pals were having a good laugh at my expense. "You okay, *petit anglo*?" they wanted to know when I was done.

I didn't mind their asking me how I was doing or their making reference to the fact that I speak English. What I didn't like was being called *petit*, which is French for "little." I guess you could say I'm sensitive about my height. I know they say a kid can still have a growth spurt when he's fifteen, or even sixteen, but frankly, I'm not holding my breath.

The best job around here is hanging up the life jackets at the end of the day.

That's because people leave all sorts of stuff in the pockets. Sunglasses, suntan lotion, gum, sometimes even cash. And get this—last week, Réal found a condom. You gotta wonder about someone who packs a condom when he goes out for a two-hour kayak trip. If you ask me, it sounds like a case for Dr. Dingle.

There's a lost-and-found bin in the office and we're supposed to put anything we find in there. Truth is, most people who come to Tadoussac are only here for a day or two. By the time they discover their sunglasses are missing, they're already on the road to someplace else.

I came up with this idea while we were hanging up the life jackets. Instead of taking stuff *out* of the pockets, I thought, why not put something *into* them? Something kind of unusual— something no one would expect to find in their pocket when they were out on the St. Lawrence.

Just when I was thinking about what I might put into one of the pockets, well, the answer just came to me. Literally. It jumped out from behind this rock where I was standing. A bullfrog. Not the best-looking specimen, either. This was a big fat guy with dark green blotches. They looked kind of like warts, only flat. It took a little effort to catch him, but I managed.

"What are you up to, Pierre?" Réal wanted to know. I could tell he was about to give me some other chore—till he spotted the bullfrog.

You should have heard Réal laugh when I slipped the frog into one of the life jackets. I didn't pick one of the orange and yellow ones. No, I picked one that was more unusual, a green and purple one. That's because I wanted to be able to keep an eye on it when the next group of kayakers went out. As for Réal, I thought he was going to keel over. I've got to admit that when one of my ideas makes someone laugh, I feel—well, I guess you could say I feel tall. Like I'm six-foot-two or something.

When Réal calmed down, I brought my finger to my lips—a sign he shouldn't tell anyone else about my little surprise. Réal nodded. Then he said something in French that I didn't quite understand, but I'd say it must've been the French equivalent of "Way to go, kid." Only this time he didn't call me "petit."

The next group of kayakers was scheduled to leave at three—after Uncle Jean gave them their basic paddling lesson. What amazes me is that he doesn't get tired of teaching people how to kayak. I mean, he goes through the exact same lesson twice a day. He makes everyone line up in rows, and he stands at the front, demonstrating with this wooden paddle: "We use our shoulders, never our wrists." Then he repeats the instruction in French. From the way he says it, you'd think he never thought of it before. I'm bored of his routine and I've only been here a week.

I felt a little bad when I saw who picked the green and purple life jacket. It was this tall, thin woman in a big straw hat that looked like a lampshade. She was with her husband—a bald guy with a beer belly. "Are you sure this is a good idea, Bill?" she was asking him when they headed down to the beach.

One thing about pranks is that they kind of have a life of their own. Once a prank gets started, you can't just call it off. Especially when you've got a guy like Réal winking at you like crazy when you push the kayak with the lady and her hubby off from the shore. "Bon voyage!" I tell them—and I can't help thinking it may be more "bon" for me, watching from the shore, than for them.

You should have heard the woman scream. It was like what they describe in mystery books as bloodcurdling. Réal and I and the rest of the crew had a perfect view. We were out on the cliffs by the beach, and Réal had brought along the binoculars from the office. I was looking through them when I saw the husband pass the suntan lotion over to the wife. Then I saw her reach into her pocket and scream.

I saw the scream before I actually heard it. I guess that has something to do with how sound travels when you're out on the water. It's a good thing kayakers sit so low in the boat. Otherwise, I think the woman might have fallen in. And then who knows what could have happened to her extremities?

Uncle Jean paddled right over to see what was happening. I saw him talking to the woman. Then he looked up at the cliffs where we were. Which is when I put down the binoculars. Only, by then I knew it was too late.

Chapter Three

One good thing about living in a B&B is that you don't get yelled at. Uncle Jean didn't even mention the frog-in-the-pocket incident. All he said was he wanted me to come out on the kayak with him at six this morning. It didn't sound like a punishment, even though getting up at 5:15 isn't exactly my idea of a good time. "It's the best time to see the whales," Uncle Jean told me when we were packing up to leave, "before those damned Zodiacs are out."

Uncle Jean is a pretty laid-back guy. The only thing that seems to set him off are those Zodiacs. They're these little inflatable motorboats that take groups of people out to see the whales. They leave all the time from the Tadoussac harbor. "They dump gasoline into the St. Lawrence, and some of them get much too close to the whales," he told me.

There's a rule up here that boats aren't supposed to get any closer than 200 meters to a whale. Uncle Jean says there are plenty of captains who ignore it. "It's difficult to enforce. Besides, there's pressure from the tourists. Everyone wants to go home and tell his neighbor, 'I got this close to a whale.'" Uncle Jean stretched out his suntanned arm to show me what he meant. "If they want to get close to a whale, they should come out in a kayak. At least we don't bother the whales when we're on the water."

Till now, Uncle Jean's been too busy to take me out in his kayak. We've had nothing but sunny days since I got here, and there've been so many customers that Uncle Jean has had to turn some away.

Even though I'm not what you'd call the country type, there's something pretty beautiful about this place, especially early in the morning. Like today, when we first looked out at the river—you can see it from the kitchen at the Whale's Tale—there was this thick layer of mist over the water. It looked like cotton candy, only gray. But by the time we got into the kayak, the mist had disappeared, and the water was so clear and blue it was hard to tell where it ended and where the sky began.

At first, neither of us said a thing. We just paddled. I have to say it felt good to be quiet for a change. The morning air kind of whipped against my face, but that felt good too.

"Keep an eye out for low-flying cormorants," Uncle Jean told me. He was sitting at the back of the kayak so he could navigate. Even though all he could see was my back, he must've known I was listening, because he kept talking.

"The birds feed on krill—the same shrimp-like creatures that whales eat. So if you spot birds flying close to the water, it's usually a good indication that there are whales close by. It's been a while, hasn't it, Pierrot, since you were out in a kayak?"

I let the "Pierrot" slip. If Uncle Jean wasn't going to get upset with me about my prank, I figured I couldn't very well complain about his calling me the name he used to call me when I was a kid. Last time I was up in Tadoussac was when I was about six. I know because there's a picture of me on the mantel at home. In it, I'm in a kayak, sitting in front, and my dad's where Uncle Jean is now. Anyway, it's so long ago all I can remember is remembering being here.

Suddenly a small brown head peeked out of the water, no more than ten feet ahead of us. "Look!" I called out, resting my paddle on the side of the kayak so I could get a better view. Whatever it was looked like a dog that had been left out in the rain. A moment later he slipped back underneath the water, leaving only some swirls on its surface.

"Harbor seal," Uncle Jean said in a low voice. "They startle easily."

He'd put his paddle down too, and for a few minutes we just floated on the still water.

"About the frog in that lady's life jacket," Uncle Jean began in the same low voice he'd used before. So he was going to confront me, after all.

This time I was glad not to have to look at him.

"I'm sorry about that, Uncle Jean," I said, trying to sound as sorry as possible. I hate apologizing—it makes me feel like an idiot who does everything wrong—but it was kind of a relief when the words were out.

"Look, your parents told me about the trouble they've been having with you. But I don't want to talk about that. When you came to stay with us in Tadoussac, it was a new start. But Pierrot, that lady could have had more than a shock. The kayak could have tipped over. Like this—"

And just then, before I could complain about being called Pierrot again, Uncle Jean did the one thing you're *never* supposed to do in a kayak. He leaned over hard, so that all his weight bore down on one side of the kayak. And Uncle Jean is big. He's over

six feet and not skinny either. I figure
he must weigh about 250 pounds.

I tried to lean into the other side of
the kayak, but it didn't make much of a
difference. We were toppling over! As
my body lurched to the left, I could feel
the cold breeze coming off the water.

We were about to capsize. Aunt
Daisy's words rang in my head, like a
song you can't forget, no matter how
hard you try. *Three minutes until you
lose sensation in your extremities.
Three minutes until*...Without meaning
to, I wriggled my fingers and toes.
While I still could.

Uncle Jean must be out of his mind.
What was he trying to do? Drown us?

All at once the kayak regained its
balance. Its prow lifted itself up from
the murky water, covering me with a
mist of watery droplets. Uncle Jean was
laughing—so loud the sound echoed in
the surrounding coves.

It was only then that I started to tremble, every part of my body shaking as if I had actually fallen into the icy waters of the St. Lawrence.

Then I heard Uncle Jean's voice. This time it was booming, not low the way it had been before. "You're not the only one who knows how to play pranks, Pierrot. When I was your age, I was pretty good at pranks myself. But there's one thing I want to tell you, and you've got to understand it—no more pranks! You got that?"

"I got—," I said, but I never finished my sentence. A huge, dark shadow was moving through the water right next to us.

"Look at that baby!" Uncle Jean whispered when the whale's head surfaced about eight feet ahead of us, and a plume of mist came spouting from its blowhole. Talk about getting close to a whale! For a second I'd been able to look right into the black of his eye.

I couldn't help feeling grateful to the creature. Thanks to him, I didn't have to make a promise—one I wasn't sure I could keep.

Chapter Four

"See you later, Petit Fou!" Uncle Jean called out as the huge whale arched its back and dove back into the icy water, leaving a thick layer of foam on the water's surface.

I knew *fou* meant someone crazy, but I didn't get the *petit* part. There was nothing small about the whale we'd just seen. He was the size of a bus.

Uncle Jean seemed to know what I was thinking. "In French, we sometimes call people—and animals—*petit* to show we like them. That whale—he's a humpback, an endangered species up here—is one of my favorites. He's been coming to Tadoussac every summer for about fifteen years."

"How do you know it's the same whale?" I asked.

"From the triangular scar underneath his tail. During mating season, male humpbacks fight for the females' attention. He must have got in someone's way," Uncle Jean explained.

"How did you get interested in whales?" I wanted to know.

The question made Uncle Jean laugh. "I guess I was born interested in whales. That's what happens when you're raised in these parts. Where I grew up, in the town of Ste. Anne de Portneuf—about an hour east of here—whales were as common as mosquitoes. Only, whales don't bite. My mother used to say she never had to sing me to sleep. The whales blowing outside my window— those were my lullabies.

"Then, when I was not much older than you are now, a teacher encouraged me to study marine biology. So I ended up at Chicoutimi University, specializing in marine mammals."

I'd never known that about Uncle Jean. I'd thought of him as a businessman—never as a scientist. Maybe my parents had mentioned it, but I wasn't paying attention. You could miss a lot that way.

There was one thing I really wanted to know. "Why are you so nuts about whales?" I asked.

This time, Uncle Jean didn't answer as quickly. Instead he took a deep breath. He exhaled with a long, slow sigh that reminded me a little of the sound Petit

Fou had made. "Why am I so nuts about whales?" he said, repeating my question. "Jeez, Pierre, I hardly know. Maybe because they're so darn big— and so darn beautiful. They make even a big guy like me feel small—which is a good thing sometimes. People get into trouble when they think they're so big the whole world revolves around them. Whales have a way of reminding us we're just a tiny part of the universe."

I thought I knew what he meant. Even Petit Fou's short visit had left me feeling that way. There's so much of the world we just don't see. I scanned the water around us, eager to spot the humpback or maybe another whale, but the water was still except for an occasional rolling wave. There were no low-flying birds in sight either.

"Paddle hard on your left," Uncle Jean directed me. "It's time to head back."

For a while I paddled so hard I didn't have the energy to ask any more questions. There was lots I still wanted to know—about Uncle Jean and about whales. If Uncle Jean was a marine biologist, why didn't he teach at a university the way my parents did? And if whales kept blowing all night, when did they sleep?

Uncle Jean must have taken a break from paddling. I could hear him opening something up. I hoped it was food. All the paddling had made me hungry. But when I tilted my head a little to see what Uncle Jean was doing, I realized he was taking out a pair of binoculars from the watertight hatch in front of him.

"Jesus Christ," I heard him mutter under his breath. "Zodiacs up ahead at three o'clock." Then he began paddling again. With both of us paddling, the kayak moved easily over the water, gliding in the direction of whatever Uncle Jean had seen.

In the distance I saw what looked like dark splotches against the horizon. But as we approached, I realized there were three Zodiacs—the little speedboats Uncle Jean hated so much. They had formed a tight circle. In the center I thought I could make out the outline of a whale.

"It's a minke," Uncle Jean told me as we moved in toward the group. "And those idiots have him cornered."

The passengers on the Zodiacs paid no attention as we paddled toward them. They were leaning out of the Zodiacs, frantically snapping photographs and shouting instructions to one another. "Get one of me with the whale, darling!" a high-pitched voice squealed.

So much for the rules. These boats couldn't have been more than a couple of meters away from the minke, who seemed to be trying to figure out how to escape. The sharp smell of gasoline hung in the air, making my nostrils burn.

Just then, one of the Zodiac captains spotted my uncle Jean. "Okay!" he called out, loud enough for the other captains to hear. "Time to move on." The captain had a shaggy gray beard and a sunburn. He had this gold ring with diamonds on his pinky finger. I noticed because the diamonds gleamed in the sunlight. I'd seen him before, only I didn't know where.

"Time to move on all right, Roméo," Uncle Jean yelled from our kayak. Considering how Uncle Jean felt about Zodiac operators, I didn't expect him to be on a first-name basis with the guy. "You know better than to get so close." Uncle Jean's voice sounded angry.

"That minke came over to see *us*," the man whose name was Roméo called out.

"I'll bet he did!" Uncle Jean didn't sound convinced.

Then I realized why the captain seemed familiar. I'd seen him at the clubhouse by the Tadoussac harbor. When I'd gone in to get sandwiches for the crew, he'd been sitting in the cafeteria, playing cards with his buddies.

The moment he had a little room to maneuver, the minke disappeared from view. There was no telling where he'd gone. Even though we weren't far from shore, I knew the water here was very deep. What other animals, I wondered, were swimming beneath us—in their own watery world?

"You okay?" I asked Uncle Jean as we made our way toward the launching dock.

"I'm okay," he muttered, but he sounded upset. "They treat the whales like performing seals. And the more people bother the whales, the less they eat—which means that, over time, their existence is endangered. Then there's all the gasoline they dump into the river. And that Roméo," he added, "we grew up together. He was as interested in whales as I was. Like I just told him, he should know better."

I made a *tsk-tsk* sound to show my disapproval, unsure what else I could say to make Uncle Jean feel better.

"They're predicting bad weather tomorrow," he said, his voice sounding a little less upset. "So when I go for groceries, I could drop you off at the Marine Mammal Interpretive Center. What do you say, Pierre?"

I'd always refused when my parents tried to talk me into going with them to one of the museums in Montreal, but this was different. This wasn't going to be about paintings or sculptures. This was about whales.

Chapter Five

The weather was bad all right. I could tell without even getting up from my bed. The sky was the color of smoke, and the pine tree outside my window was tottering in the wind like an old drunk. There were none of the usual morning sounds in the house. The radio wasn't blaring, the coffee machine wasn't gurgling, and there wasn't the usual chatter of guests as they lined up for the downstairs bathroom. Everyone seemed to be sleeping in—something that didn't happen much in Tadoussac.

But I was wide awake. So I slipped on my jeans and sweatshirt and tiptoed down the winding wooden staircase to the main floor. A Scrabble board had been left out on the table, the game still unfinished. The word *temptation* was spelled out across the middle of the board.

Aunt Daisy and Uncle Jean didn't have a bolt on their front door the way we did in Montreal. I unlatched the screen door and headed for the small patio at the front of the house. There weren't any chairs—only this small, bright pink bench people used when they put on their boating shoes. I sat down and looked out at the St. Lawrence. Today, there was no mist over the water—if there had been a mist, it would have been blown away by the gusting wind.

Even without binoculars I could see the waves tumbling toward the shore with a force I hadn't seen before. In the distance I spotted a huge cargo ship moving a little unsteadily across the water. I didn't want to imagine what it would be like to be out in a kayak in these conditions. Uncle Jean had warned me that the St. Lawrence was moody. "It's beautiful all right," he'd told me, "but she can be like this girlfriend I had before I met Daisy. Calm one minute, wild the next. A guy never knows where he stands with a woman like that."

Just then I heard the squeal of bicycle brakes. Whoever it was had stopped at the gray-shingled house next to the B&B. Just as I was craning my neck for a closer look, someone tapped on my shoulder.

"Bonjour, you. It's me—Rosalie," a girl's voice said.

I turned around to see a smiling, freckled face between two long brown braids. "I'm Pete," I said, extending my hand, "er, Pierre."

"Pete," the girl repeated slowly. From the way she said it, you could tell she hadn't ever heard the name before. "I am Rosalie Marchand," she said slowly. "I live next door."

"I figured that."

"You figured?" Rosalie said. "Excuse me, but my English is not very good."

"I figured you live next door since that's where you parked your bike."

"Oh," said Rosalie, brightening. "I see."

"How come we haven't met before?" I asked.

"We were away, visiting my grandfather in Chicoutimi. We returned home only last night. My parents told me you were here, staying with Jean and Daisy. You got in trouble in Montreal, didn't you?"

I didn't know what to say to that.

Rosalie kept right on talking. Not the shy type, you could say. "No kayaking today, I suppose," she said, gesturing toward the water. "What are we going to do?"

"We?" I repeated, a little surprised. Maybe this was a Tadoussac thing. In Montreal, people didn't go around making plans with people they'd just met. "Uncle Jean is supposed to drop me off at the interpretive center later," I told her.

"Just ring the bell before you leave. I'll come." And with a toss of her braids, Rosalie disappeared into the wind.

Uncle Jean and Aunt Daisy seemed glad when I said I'd met Rosalie—and that she'd invited herself to come along to the center. They left us at the top of the long, winding parking lot. "We'll do our groceries, have a café au lait in town and pick you up at two," Aunt

Daisy said, checking her watch as she slammed the van door shut behind us.

"It's busier than usual," Rosalie said as we paid our admission. "When it's sunny, there's hardly anyone here." The displays were in French, but when the clerk heard us speaking English, she offered us two English booklets. "He'll take one, not me," said Rosalie. "I speak French." You could tell she was pleased that the woman had thought she was English.

Rosalie knew her way around. "You've got to listen to this," she said, grabbing my elbow and leading me toward the back of the main exhibit room. Once we got there, she reached to the wall for a set of headphones and shoved them over my ears as if they were earmuffs. Through what sounded like an ocean of bubbles, I could hear a series of strange high-pitched whistles, like nothing I'd ever heard before.

"Whales," Rosalie explained excitedly when I took off the headphones. "They live in a world of sound. Scientists say whales use their own language to communicate. Cool, no? Now come and see what happens when a calf—that's a baby whale—is born." Rosalie dragged me to another booth where we watched a video of a calf swimming up to the water's surface to take its first breath.

"For humans, breathing is an instinct. But not for whales," Rosalie said. "They have to remember to breathe. At night, only half their brain goes to sleep. The other half stays awake and reminds them to breathe." Rosalie was talking awfully fast now, as if her words were having trouble keeping up with everything she wanted to say. Still, I was glad she'd answered the question I'd wanted to ask Uncle Jean—about whether whales ever got to sleep.

It was hard to see what was going on at the next station because there were so many kids crowded round it, making noisy panting sounds. Lucky for me, I had my personal tour guide. "Belugas can hold their breath for up to twenty minutes," Rosalie explained. "And sperm whales can hold theirs for up to an hour and a half. How long can you hold yours?"

So that's what all the kids were doing—trying to see how long they could hold their breath. There was even a computerized timer to help with the calculation. "My turn, my turn," I said as I elbowed my way past the crowd.

Rosalie had been in charge so far—dragging me here and there and explaining stuff—but I was about to become the center of attention. A warm, familiar feeling came over me, as if I was about to go on stage.

"Think of me as a whale," I said, inhaling deeply through my nostrils. And then I held my breath—so long that I felt my cheeks puff up and my face turn hot, and then hotter.

The kids I'd pushed out of the way were looking at me, their eyes widening in surprise. I turned to look at Rosalie next. She'd covered her mouth with one hand.

And then I tumbled to the floor, making a loud thud as I hit the ground. I even rolled around, letting my head drop from left to right, just to add to the effect. "Quick! Call the doctor!" I heard Rosalie yell. One little girl started to cry, tears running down her cheeks.

The kid's crying got to me. Slowly, like a rag doll, I picked myself up from the ground, pretending to be a little groggy. Everyone's eyes were on me, including those of the clerk who'd given me the English booklet and who had rushed over to see what was going on.

"Gotcha!" I said with a laugh as I stood up.

But no one seemed to know what "gotcha" meant. The clerk looked confused; the little girl was still crying. As for Rosalie, she'd stomped out of the room without looking back.

Chapter Six

Rosalie didn't go very far. I could see her standing on the balcony that looked out over the water. I thought I'd give her a few minutes, but she didn't come back inside. She didn't even turn to see if I was watching her. I figured that meant it was up to me to go get her. Not that I planned on apologizing or anything.

"I was just kidding around," I told her. Actually I told it to her back, since she was staring at the water—or pretending to. All I could see were those long braids of hers dangling on either side of her head, but I could picture the rest of her face as if I was looking right at it. The big smile, the freckles, the blue eyes. I had to admit she was kind of pretty, even if she did talk too much.

But she wasn't talking now. She was staring out at the water as if it contained some secret message only she could understand.

"My uncle says the St. Lawrence reminds him of this girlfriend he once had. She was really moody," I said, trying to make conversation.

"This isn't the St. Lawrence anymore," she said, still without turning around. "It's the Saguenay River. The Saguenay is a saltwater fjord, the largest in Eastern Canada. It empties into the

St. Lawrence." She was starting to sound like a tour guide again, but at least she was talking to me. Well, sort of.

"Look out over there," I said, "at about eleven o'clock." From here the water looked very black, and I'd spotted some white blotches bobbing up to the surface.

"Belugas," she said as she turned to the left. This time her voice sounded excited. There were three or four of them. Unlike minkes, who tended to travel alone or in pairs, belugas, my uncle had told me, were more sociable, often traveling in large groups or pods. They were the most endangered of all the whales in this area. "Belugas are the only whales that stay here all year long," Rosalie said.

"Where do the rest go?" I asked. I couldn't tell for sure whether she was still mad at me, but I didn't think so.

"No one knows," she said. Her voice sounded sad. "Why do you do things like that?" she asked suddenly.

"Like what?" I asked, though I knew she wasn't talking about whales. I was beginning to notice that Rosalie had a habit of just changing the subject out of nowhere.

"Like pretending you choked to death," she said. The last couple of words sounded as if she were spitting them out.

"It was just a prank."

"A prank?" She didn't seem to know the word, and I didn't know how to say "prank" in French.

"You know, kind of a joke."

"Why do you do them—pranks?" Rosalie asked. You could tell she was trying out the word for the first time.

"I don't know," I said. It was true— I didn't know why I pulled pranks.

"My mother says it's probably because you lack attention," she blurted out.

"What does your mother know about it?" I asked. I was beginning to get pissed off. What business did Rosalie's mother have trying to figure out why I pulled pranks? I'd never even met the woman, but I could tell I wouldn't like her.

"Jean and Daisy told her what happened to you at school. How you got kicked out for saying those things on the radio about—" She stopped herself, as if she knew she'd said too much.

"You know about that?" I asked.

"Everyone knows. Tadoussac's a small place," she said.

That made me wonder who else knew. Did Réal and the other guys on the work crew know? Was that why the lady in the cheese shop gave me a disapproving look whenever I came in with Uncle Jean?

"Maybe you do pranks when you feel angry," Rosalie suggested.

"You don't *do* pranks—you pull them," I said, correcting her English.

I guess right then I *was* feeling angry. Who did this girl think she was, trying to figure me out? And there I was, thinking I'd come to Tadoussac with my past behind me, only to find out that everyone here knew about the trouble I'd gotten into at home. Darn right I felt angry.

"It does get me angry when you talk to me like I'm on a tour—and you're the tour guide. And it gets me angry when you drag me around from one exhibit to the next. Maybe you're right, maybe I *do* pull pranks when I'm angry," I said, feeling kind of embarrassed when I realized how loudly I was talking. This middle-aged couple standing at the other end of the balcony were giving me funny looks. I hoped they didn't understand English.

I couldn't help wondering, though, about what Rosalie had said. I'd been angry at Mr. Quincy about the detention. On the other hand, I hadn't been angry at that woman who found the frog in the life jacket. I hadn't even known she'd be the one to take that particular life jacket. But maybe I'd been angry at Réal and the other guys on the crew for giving me all the rotten jobs and for treating me like an outsider.

"It's after two," Rosalie said. "Your Uncle Jean and Aunt Daisy will be waiting. Let's go," she said, taking my arm. "Oh, excuse me," she added shyly, dropping my arm. "I forgot you don't like being dragged around."

"That's okay," I said, hooking my arm through hers. "But Rosalie, there's one thing. Don't say anything to Jean and Daisy about the prank, okay?"

"Okay," she said, smiling up at me. "But no more pranks, okay?"

"No more pranks!" I said with a laugh.

The van was waiting at the top of the parking lot. To my surprise, Uncle Jean and Aunt Daisy didn't ask about our visit to the center. When we slid into the backseat, they were in the middle of what sounded like an important conversation.

"I can't say no," Uncle Jean was saying. "It's too big an opportunity."

"But we don't have enough employees to staff an overnight trip," Aunt Daisy said. "And I can't spare you at the B&B. It's our busiest season."

Uncle Jean turned around to look first at me and then at Rosalie. "I may need some help from the two of you."

"Sure," I said.

"Bien sûr," Rosalie said at the same time.

"I've been asked to organize an overnight kayak trip. I'd like you two to go along. If your parents agree, Rosalie, you and Pierre can set up the tents, and prepare meals."

It sounded like fun. And it didn't hurt when Uncle Jean said he'd pay us each double the minimum wage for our trouble.

"Besides yourselves and Réal, there'll be four people going on the trip," Uncle Jean explained as we drove back along the winding highway that led toward the Whale's Tale. "They should be waiting at the B&B when we get there."

Aunt Daisy nudged Uncle Jean as the van pulled up in the driveway. "You'd better warn the kids about the names," she said. From where I was sitting, I could see Aunt Daisy suck in her cheeks. My mom does that when she's trying not to laugh.

Uncle Jean turned around to face us. Though he was grinning, his voice was serious. "Your Aunt Daisy's right. There is something I'd better warn you about. Those four people going on the trip— they're all named Mike."

Chapter Seven

"Pleased to meet you. I'm Mike," said a tall red-headed guy standing in the doorway at the B&B. He took my hand and pumped it hard. "This here's my buddy, Mike," he said, gesturing to another guy, who was crouched on the floor, surrounded by a mound of clothing. He seemed to be looking for something inside his suitcase.

"Found it," the second Mike said as he turned to greet us, the thing he'd been looking for—a huge bottle of insect repellant—in one hand. As he stood up, he swatted his own arm. "Gotcha," he said, examining the bloody remains of a mosquito on his fingertips. From the look on his face, you'd think he'd defeated some mortal enemy.

"I'm Mike," announced a third man as he walked out of the bathroom and adjusted his glasses. "I'm his brother-in-law," he said, lifting his chin in the direction of the first Mike, the one with the red hair.

Just as I was thinking I'd never seen so many Mikes in one place, another one came down the stairs. I figured he was a year or two older than me. And because he was tall, with red hair and wide shoulders, I had a feeling he was the first Mike's son.

"That there's my boy, Mike—"

"Junior," I said, finishing the first Mike's sentence.

"It's one of the most common names in the world," the Mike with the glasses explained. "Of course, there are variations—Mike, Michael, Miguel…"

"Michel," added Rosalie, who was standing in the hallway.

I couldn't help thinking that the possibilities for pranks here were endless. I could get up in the middle of the night and yell "Mike!" to see how many of them answered. Or I could make each of them a nametag with the name Mike on it. "Just so I can tell you guys apart," I'd say. That'd definitely be fun.

Then I remembered my promise to Rosalie. She'd kept her end of the deal by not telling Uncle Jean and Aunt Daisy about what had happened at the interpretive center. But maybe, I thought, pulling pranks was just part of who I was. Maybe I couldn't help pulling pranks any more than Mike Junior could help having red hair, no matter what Rosalie and her mom had to say about it.

The Mikes were spending the night at the B&B. If the sky was clear, we'd head out first thing in the morning. Our destination was Ile des Lièvres, a small island a couple of kilometers from the mouth of the Saguenay.

Réal dropped by after dinner to review the route with Uncle Jean. I watched them hunched over a map of the area. "As long as it's not too windy, the only tricky part is crossing between the ferries," I overheard Uncle Jean say.

During the summer months, ferries leave every twenty minutes to cross the Saguenay to Tadoussac. There are ferries at night and in winter too, but they're less frequent. We'd need to time things just right so that none of our kayaks were caught in the path of the huge passenger boats.

"You'll need to pack light," Uncle Jean told the Mikes when he joined them later around the fireplace in the living room. "There isn't much storage space in a kayak. And there are plenty of necessities to carry—tents, sleeping bags, food and water." He and Réal had already begun to organize supplies. The corridor between the kitchen and the living room was lined with cardboard boxes piled high with some of the stuff Uncle Jean had described. I spotted a box of dry cereal, several packets of noodles and a box of granola bars. From the looks of it, Rosalie and I wouldn't be doing any gourmet cooking.

Mike Junior slept on a cot in my room. His feet hung over the end of the mattress, but he didn't complain.

I thought he was okay, except for his snoring. After a while, when the noise really started to get to me, I took one of the pillows from my bed and threw it at him. It landed—bull's eye—right over his mouth. I was glad he didn't wake up—and that he quit snoring.

Kayaking, especially in the choppy waters of the St. Lawrence and the Saguenay, can be hard work. In all, we were four kayaks. Rosalie and I had led the group out of the Tadoussac harbour. A cruise ship was pulling out at the same time. Several passengers on the deck waved as they passed us. Réal, the only one in our group in a single kayak, had stayed toward the rear so he could keep an eye on the rest of us. Though the sky was clear, there was some wind. Luckily, it was moving in the same direction we were.

This time I sat in the stern. Rosalie's braids were tucked under her sun hat.

As we rounded the first cove, we reached the confluence—the point where the St. Lawrence and the Saguenay meet. From here, the St. Lawrence looked bigger than ever. I tried to imagine what it must have been like to be one of the early explorers, arriving in this area for the first time. Though the St. Lawrence dwarfed the Saguenay, I knew that the quick-moving waters of the fjord could be just as dangerous.

Réal whistled—a sign we were to wait for him to catch up with us. "Got any snacks?" Mike Junior called out as the kayak he and his dad were in approached ours. I passed him a granola bar I'd tucked into the pocket of my life jacket the night before.

"Sure is beautiful out here," Mike Junior said, unpacking the bar. The wrapper flapped in the wind. For a minute I thought he was going to toss the piece of foil into the water, but he seemed to change his mind, stuffing it instead into one of the pockets on his life jacket.

Réal pulled up just after the other kayaks. "Okay," he said, checking his watch, "we should be at the ferry crossing in about ten minutes—which gives us another ten minutes before the next ferry. Do you want to try to do it, or should we take a break and wait till after the next ferry crosses?"

The Mikes exchanged looks. "Let's go for it," Mike Junior's dad announced. Even after just a morning out on the water, his face was sunburned a fiery red.

"The wind is with us," said Réal, eyeing some bushes near the shoreline. Like the foil wrapper Mike Junior had been holding in his hands, the bushes were blowing west—the same direction we were heading down the fjord. "Let's go then," Réal announced. He pressed the end of his paddle against the back of our kayak—his signal that we were setting off.

Across the channel, a ferry was docking. In the distance we could see cars disembarking, and along the nearby road a long snaking line of cars and trucks waiting to get on. Keeping my shoulders straight, I used my forearms to paddle ahead. Tiny droplets of sweat glistened on the back of Rosalie's neck. She hummed as she paddled, but I couldn't make out the tune.

Just then a gust of wind lifted Rosalie's hat from her head. "I liked that hat," I heard her mutter.

Without thinking, I let my paddle slide and reached into the air for the hat.

"Don't do that," Rosalie said in a voice I hadn't heard her use before. The hat flew off, close to the water, like one of the cormorants Uncle Jean had told me about.

Rosalie's hat was lost, but at least the kayak was stable. If I'd reached any farther forward, we might have tipped. I couldn't help thinking of the woman I'd pranked the other day. Even though I was wearing two layers over my wetsuit, my body felt chilled.

The hat took off into the sky like a balloon. Then something suddenly occurred to me. Rosalie's hat was blowing east, not west. The wind had changed direction.

"Pierre! Rosalie!" Réal's shouts echoed across the water. When we turned to look at him, he was pointing at the ferry. It was headed right for us.

Even if the ferry captain had seen us, there wasn't much he could have done. The ferry was attached to underwater cables that pulled it from one side of the Saguenay to the other.

For a second we didn't do anything except stare. The ferry was massive.

"Pierre! Rosalie!" Réal shouted again. This time he pointed to a small cove behind us.

"Paddle backward!" Rosalie and I yelled to each other at the same time, and together we reversed the kayak.

"Holy cow," Mike Junior's dad said, using the back of one hand to mop his forehead as we pulled into the cove.

"Listen," Réal said, his voice a little jittery. "The wind changing like that gave us all a scare. Maybe we should go back to Tadoussac," he said, looking first at Rosalie and me, and then at the Mikes.

"We're okay," Rosalie said, "aren't we?"

I nodded in agreement.

"All right, but with the wind in front of us, we'll have to paddle hard to cross the ferry line," Réal said.

We made amazing time. Without a ferry staring us in the eye, the paddling seemed easy.

Once we were out of the ferry's range, we slowed down. The sun's rays warmed our skin. We let our kayak float toward the others. Rosalie passed out juice boxes.

"On a normal day it would take two hours of paddling to reach Ile des Lièvres. But it'll take longer today," Réal explained.

It's easy to lose track of time when you're in a kayak. There's something hypnotic about watching your paddle scoop water and then feeling it fly into the air behind you in a cool spray.

There was lots to do once we reached the grassy island. The kayaks had to be dragged up the beach so they wouldn't be pulled out by the current. Mike Junior helped Rosalie and me set up tents and build a fire. Supper was baked potatoes and steaks, which Uncle Jean had packed on ice.

Mike Junior hung around as Rosalie and I chopped vegetables for a salad.

I knew he wasn't interested in cooking, but I thought he might be interested in Rosalie. Rosalie didn't pay any particular attention to him. "I think I'll go to my tent and read," she announced after we'd set the picnic table.

Mike Junior was rolling his shoulders backward. "That kayaking's some workout," he said, curling his biceps as he spoke.

I bet he does weights, I thought, looking down at my own arms and wondering if, by the end of the summer, there was any chance they'd get that ripply look Mike Junior's had. As I looked toward my fingertips, the row of colorful kayaks down by the beach caught my eye. Turned on their backs, they looked like small whales.

"Just imagine," I said to myself, but loud enough for Mike Junior to hear, "what a panic everyone would be in if the kayaks disappeared. We'd be stranded!"

Mike Junior stopped flexing his muscles and looked right at me. "Has anyone ever told you you're brilliant, Pete? Absolutely brilliant?"

Just then, part of me did feel brilliant.

But another part of me felt stupid—absolutely stupid.

Chapter Eight

It was nearly midnight when we zipped up our tents. Réal and the Mikes were a little tipsy. Uncle Jean had packed two of those cardboard boxes of wine, the kind people serve at parties. "I don't drink that plonk!" the Mike who wasn't related to the other Mikes said when Rosalie and I put the boxes out on the picnic table.

It was kind of hard to take him seriously considering the get-up he was wearing: this green helmet with a huge piece of mosquito netting attached to it. He looked like a cross between a soldier and a bride.

"Plonk?" Rosalie said. This was obviously another new word for her.

"It means he doesn't like it," I explained under my breath.

Plonk or no plonk, both boxes were empty before dessert. Rosalie and I were supposed to stick to juice, but when the others weren't looking, I downed a camping cup full of wine. It felt warm as it trickled down my throat.

We'd set up the tents in a semicircle up a small hill from the beach. Each tent was a short walk from the outhouse—a wooden shack surrounded by fir trees. We were two to a tent, except for Rosalie, who had a tent to herself.

I was sharing with Mike Junior. At first we just lay in our sleeping bags, looking out the mesh window at the stars. Since I didn't have a pillow, I was trying to figure out what I could throw at him if he started snoring again.

He broke the silence. "So when are we hiding the kayaks?" he whispered.

"Huh?" I said, playing dumb. Jeez, I thought to myself, I wish I'd never come up with the scheme. All I wanted was to get some sleep—and stay out of trouble. But I was beginning to suspect Mike Junior was the kind of guy who'd be hard to stop once he got an idea into his head, even if the idea was mine.

"Don't you want to sleep?" I asked, trying to sound really tired.

"I'm wide awake," Mike Junior said.

The thing I was beginning to learn about pranks is that once you dream one up, it's hard to stop. So I tried another tactic. "Mike," I said, "maybe hiding the kayaks isn't such a great idea."

"You've got to be kidding, Pete. Think how much fun it'll be to see Réal's face when he thinks they're missing. The guy will have a cow."

It *was* kind of fun to imagine the look on Réal's face. But I also had a feeling Réal wasn't the sort of person who'd appreciate being pranked. "He'll be really pissed off when he figures out who did it," I told Mike Junior.

"No way," he said. "Your uncle's his boss—he can't get mad at you."

"Hey, you two are making too much noise!" It was Rosalie, speaking in a stage whisper from the next tent. I wondered whether she was more upset about being awakened, or about the fact that we were leaving her out of our conversation.

"We're sorry," I whispered back. My theory that she was upset about being left out must have been right, because a minute later she was standing outside our tent, dressed in a flowery flannel house-coat and fuzzy pink slippers that didn't look like they were meant for camping.

"What's going on, anyway?" she demanded.

"Nothing," I said. "We're trying to sleep."

You could tell she didn't believe me.

"Want to come in for a game of cards?" Mike Junior asked, sitting up in his sleeping bag and using his hand to comb the hair out of his face.

"No thanks, I'm dead tired," she said as she turned her back and shuffled back toward her tent.

"Did you catch those slippers? Pretty sexy!" Mike Junior said with a laugh, but I was pretending to be asleep. It's a good thing Rosalie woke up, I thought, or I might have had to move those kayaks after all. I remember having this relieved kind of feeling as I dozed off—kind of like I was supposed to have an organ removed, and at the last minute, the doctor changed his mind and said I didn't need the operation.

I didn't sleep long. The sky was still black when I felt Mike Junior tapping my shoulder. "Let's go!" he whispered.

For some reason I can't quite explain, I got up and tugged on my sweats. Maybe I was too tired to argue. "Shh," he said, holding one finger to his lips as we passed Rosalie's tent.

We made our way past the other tents and down the gravel path to the beach. The tide was much higher than when we'd docked. Now the beach was more than half-covered by water. It was a good thing we'd put the kayaks as high as we did or they would have been carried off by the current.

Silently, Mike Junior took one end of the closest kayak, and I took the other.

Emptied of its contents, the kayak, which was made of lightweight fiberglass, was easy to move. We headed for a small area nearby, overgrown with bushes and trees. The bushes scratched against my ankles. Nobody would spot the kayaks here.

A loud rumble startled us. At first I thought it was snoring. Maybe it was Mike Junior's dad, and snoring was another thing they had in common. But we were too far from the tents to hear anyone snore. Then I heard the noise again. Mike Junior and I let the kayak we were carrying drop to the ground.

The noise—it sounded now like a loud bleating sound—was coming from the water. As I turned to look in the direction of the Saguenay, I saw something huge and black. Against the dark horizon it looked as big as a mountain. But something told me it was a whale. Something else told me he was in trouble—big trouble.

Chapter Nine

Another thing I've learned about pranks is sometimes something really important happens, and you forget all about whatever pranks you've got planned. Which is what happened to us. We'd only moved the first kayak when we heard the whale making that bleating noise.

We rushed down to the water, shining our flashlights in front of us.

It was a whale all right—floating on the water's surface, only a couple of meters from the beach. When we directed our flashlights closer to his body, we both gasped. Even in the dark, the surrounding water had an unmistakable red tinge. "He's bleeding," I told Mike Junior.

I could tell from the fleshy knobs on top of his head near his blowhole, and from his long flippers, that this was a humpback. Because of the way he was lying, the area beneath his tail was exposed. That's when I saw it— the triangular scar—the one Uncle Jean had told me about. "Petit Fou!" I called out, and for a second I thought I saw the giant tail quiver.

"You *know* him?" Mike Junior asked.

"I've seen him out on the St. Lawrence."

"What do you think happened?" he wanted to know.

"My uncle told me humpbacks can get into fights—during mating season. But it's past mating season. I can't figure what—"

A loud whirring sound, coming from somewhere out on the water, interrupted me. I looked up. I could barely make out the shape of a boat. "It's a Zodiac," I told Mike Junior. "But what's it doing out now?"

Then, just like that, the answer came to me. "I'll bet Petit Fou got bashed by that Zodiac." A cold anger rose in me. Petit Fou had stopped bleating, but he was breathing fast, his huge whale body heaving up and down. I'd never heard a volcano about to explode, but I imagined that was what it would sound like.

"What do we do now?" Mike Junior asked.

"We'd better wake the others," I told him. It was hard to turn our backs on Petit Fou, but we had to.

Réal and Mike Junior's dad were already halfway out of their tent. "What's the racket?" Réal asked, rubbing his eyes. "Who's crazy enough to be out on a boat at this hour?"

"There's a whale," I managed to tell them, though it felt like my breath was caught in my throat. "He's bleeding!"

"Bleeding?" Réal seemed shocked. The sky had grown a little brighter, and I watched his face turn pale.

Rosalie and the others were up now too. "A whale—bleeding," I heard voices say as they unzipped their tents and slipped on their sneakers.

Rosalie didn't say a word, but her look told me she thought Mike Junior and I were somehow responsible for whatever trouble there was.

"We'd better radio my uncle. He might be able to get a veterinarian from the interpretive center," I said to Réal as we started down the path. I knew

Réal had a two-way radio with him. He needed it in case any of us got into trouble—or if one of the kayaks got damaged. Suddenly I remembered my latest prank. For a second I felt a little guilty—but there was no time, I told myself, to think about that now.

When we got to the beach, Réal's attention was so focused on the whale that he didn't notice the missing kayak.

"I think it's Petit Fou," I told him.

"Did you see the scar?" Réal asked, without lifting his eyes from the whale.

"Yup," I said, "underneath his tail and shaped like a triangle."

The radio made a crackling sound when Réal turned it on and passed it to me. "Uncle Jean? It's me, Pete. We've got a big problem. No, we're all fine. It's Petit Fou. I think a Zodiac hit him."

Even through the static, I could hear my uncle swearing at the other end. In both languages.

It was hard to make out Uncle Jean's next words, but I could have guessed what they'd be. "Did you recognize the Zodiac?" he wanted to know.

"It was dark," I said, wishing I had a better answer.

"My uncle's going to the interpretive center," I told the others when I put down the radio. "When there's more light, he'll try to get a helicopter over here. In the meantime, he says to keep Petit Fou wet."

"We can use that bucket," Réal suggested, lifting his eyes to the spot where we'd had dinner a few hours before. "Hey, where's the other kayak?" His voice sounded more tired than upset.

"Uh, it's up in the bushes," Mike Junior said, as if the bushes were a perfectly normal place to keep a kayak. "It was Pete's idea," he added.

I decided not to hang around for the rest of the conversation. Instead I made a beeline for the bucket. When I turned back to the water, I spotted Rosalie sitting near the shore on a moss-covered boulder. I could tell she was ignoring me. Her mouth was wide open, as if she wasn't paying any attention to me or Réal or Mike Junior.

I followed her gaze out to the water. Petit Fou was still there, floating heavily on the surface, his breath quick and labored. But he wasn't alone. Surrounding him were four other humpbacks—three adults and a calf. I hadn't been the only one communicating. Except Petit Fou hadn't needed a radio to call for help.

Chapter Ten

"The fact that sound travels four times faster underwater than it does in air helps whales communicate with each other," Rosalie was saying as we waded out into the Saguenay and took turns emptying the bucket of water onto Petit Fou. The water was so cold it made our legs ache, but it felt good to do something for Petit Fou.

Rosalie was back in know-it-all mode. Still, you have to admit it was pretty cool about the other humpbacks coming to keep Petit Fou company. I mean, it really seemed like he *had* communicated with them.

If I were a whale, I'd be a humpback. That's because they're showmen, known for diving and slapping their flippers. But the four who'd come to hang with Petit Fou seemed to be lying low.

The Mikes had changed into warm clothes and wading boots. "We'll take over," Mike Junior's dad called out as he came down the hill. "You kids better warm up," he added, tossing a couple of sleeping bags our way.

Rosalie and I went to sit by the fire Mike Junior and Réal had lit. I meant to watch the humpbacks, but soon I felt my chin drop to my chest and my head swing to one side. As I dozed off, my mind went back to the pool of blackish red water Mike Junior and I had seen when we'd first come down to the river. And then, still in my half-sleep, I remembered the whirring sound of the Zodiac's motor as it zoomed off into the dark. Only, this time I saw something: a white flag hanging from the boat's stern.

"It had a white flag," I muttered. My own words woke me up.

"What?" Rosalie asked. My head had been slumped on her shoulder. She couldn't have been comfortable, but it was nice of her not to have pushed me away.

"The Zodiac—the one that took off when Mike Junior and I came down to the shore. It had a white flag."

"White flag?" Rosalie said, turning my words into a question. "It must belong to Leblanc. He owns a fleet of Zodiacs, and they all have white flags. Just like his name, Leblanc—which means the 'white one.'"

"I've seen him. He and Uncle Jean grew up together."

"They did?" Rosalie sounded surprised.

With the other humpbacks nearby, Petit Fou seemed to settle down. But the pool of reddish water grew around him. "It's a good thing his blowhole is out of the water," I heard Réal say as he and the others took turns dumping more water onto Petit Fou's huge body.

The rest of the night passed in much the same way. Half-asleep, half-awake, we kept an eye on Petit Fou, getting up every twenty minutes or so to relieve the others. What sleep we got was interrupted by Petit Fou's occasional bleating, and by the whooshing sound of the other humpbacks coming up for air.

The whir of a helicopter told us it was a new day. Uncle Jean's eyes were small and red; his clothes, rumpled. "This is Chantal Youville," he said, introducing the pilot, who also turned out to be the veterinarian.

"Pleased to meet you," Dr. Youville said, without bothering to look at any of us as she rushed out of the helicopter. She reached into the back of the helicopter for her backpack and sprinted down the beach toward Petit Fou. Uncle Jean followed, stopping only to rumple my hair as he passed.

We crowded around Dr. Youville as she examined Petit Fou. "Looks like his tail was caught in a motor. Pierre," she said, gesturing toward me, "get the syringe from my backpack. It's already loaded with antibiotics."

I'll never complain about needles again, I thought as I passed her the biggest syringe I'd ever seen.

"It's mostly used for horses," Dr. Youville explained as she waded out into the water, holding the syringe like a machine gun.

"Will it hurt?" Rosalie asked.

"I doubt it," Dr. Youville replied. "And once the antibiotics take effect, Petit Fou should be able to heal without developing an infection. If he's strong enough to swim—provided that doesn't take too long—he may survive. The water is the best place for a whale to heal."

I winced as she injected the antibiotics into the whale's belly. The others who'd been standing around all took a step back as the syringe pierced Petit Fou's flesh. I tried to imagine the antibiotics working their way into Petit Fou's system, penetrating the blubber and then traveling to all of his organs— and, of course, to his damaged tail.

But there wasn't time for imagining. Rosalie nudged my arm. "How are we going to catch Leblanc?" she whispered.

Chapter Eleven

Why do girls always order salad? I knew better than to ask Rosalie, especially since I wasn't in the mood for some lecture about vitamins and fiber.

"I'll have a burger and fries," I told the lady when it was my turn to order. The fries were way better at the chip wagon, but that was on the outskirts of town. There was nothing special about the food at the clubhouse cafeteria, but you couldn't beat its location—smack in the middle of the dock in downtown Tadoussac.

I scanned the room and led Rosalie to a small table by the window. As I put down my tray, I nodded at the group of men sitting nearby, playing cards. Outside, tourists were lining up for the giant tour boats. Strange to think that just three days ago we'd pulled up here in our kayaks after the overnight trip.

As Dr. Youville had predicted, Petit Fou's bleeding had stopped. Last we'd heard, the whale was just beginning to swim out into the shallow water. Dr. Youville and another vet from the interpretive center were monitoring Petit Fou's progress.

"Are you and your uncle still fighting?" Rosalie asked. She was leaning in so close our heads nearly touched.

"I don't want to talk about it," I muttered, backing away from Rosalie. I turned around to check that no one was listening to our conversation. A couple of the card players looked away before our eyes could meet.

"My mother says it helps to talk things through," Rosalie persisted.

"Your mother says a lot of stuff." I rolled my eyes to indicate I didn't think much of Rosalie's mother. "Besides, I believe in doing things—not just talking about doing things. If you really want to know"—and here I let my voice drop a little—"that's the worst part about living with someone like Uncle Jean."

Rosalie nodded, and when, a second later, she made a clucking sound, I couldn't help thinking of Dr. Dingle.

"Uncle Jean talks nonstop about all these plans he's got to expand his business. He says he wants to design his own website and increase his prices.

The problem is—all he ever does is talk!" I continued.

"But your Uncle Jean is a good person. And he loves whales," Rosalie said softly. You could tell she was trying to calm me down, only this time, she didn't cluck.

"What's the good of being good?" I said, and I could hear the disgust in my own voice. "If Uncle Jean was smarter, he'd remember he's got bills to pay, and that whale watching isn't about saving the world. It's about making money to pay those bills."

Rosalie looked me straight in the eye. "You can't mean that," she said, her voice rising.

"I do mean it, Rosalie. Sometimes I think you're as bad as Uncle Jean. Next thing I know you'll be telling me what to have for lunch, where to hang my towel, and how to line up the kayaks. Twenty-two more days till I go home to

Montreal, and I'm not sure I'm going to last!" I pounded my fist on the table for emphasis.

Rosalie stood up. Her salad was still uneaten. "I don't know if I can be friends with someone like you," she said, her lower lip trembling as she spoke. Then, without looking back, she headed for the door.

I took a big bite of my hamburger.

"It sounds like you could use some help," a gravelly voice said. I didn't have to look up to know whom the voice belonged to. It was Roméo Leblanc. He'd been playing cards at the next table. I'd spotted him—and that diamond pinky ring of his—when I was looking for a place to sit.

"What do you mean?" I asked, looking up at him. At the slamming of the door we both turned to look outside. There was Rosalie, storming by, her braids flapping in the wind.

Leblanc turned back toward me so that only I noticed when Rosalie suddenly spun around. As my eyes met hers, Rosalie mouthed the words to a message: "One last prank!"

Chapter Twelve

Of course, the real reason Leblanc offered me a job was that he wanted to annoy Uncle Jean. I could tell by the way his eyes gleamed when he came over in the clubhouse. "I could use some help with my boats. And from the sounds of it, you could use a new job," he'd said, without bothering to pretend he hadn't been listening in.

Things went even better than Rosalie and I planned. For one thing, Leblanc didn't mind when I said I wanted to work at least another week for Uncle Jean. "I owe him that. But he only needs me during the day. I could be at the dock by six," I told him.

The work wasn't glamorous— sweeping out Zodiacs and emptying trash bins—but it was a way to learn about Leblanc's operation. If Rosalie and I were going to convince park officials that one of Leblanc's Zodiacs had injured Petit Fou, we needed proof of two things: that his Zodiacs were out late at night on the Saguenay and that they got too close to the whales. If we could prove this, we hoped park officials would confiscate his license.

For now, I decided not to tell Uncle Jean and Aunt Daisy what Rosalie and I were up to. They wouldn't like it. Luckily, they didn't get suspicious when

I said I'd be hanging out by the dock after dinner.

The hardest part wasn't working two jobs; it was that I couldn't spend much time with Rosalie. If we wanted our plan to work, we had to make it look like we'd stopped being friends. The only time we talked was first thing in the morning, when we'd meet for a few minutes on the pink bench outside the Whale's Tale.

"Leblanc wants me to work late tonight and tomorrow," I told Rosalie as I sipped my hot chocolate. "I've got a camera. Did you remember the tape recorder?"

It was Rosalie's idea that I should get Leblanc to admit he sometimes took clients whale watching at night. "You could tape him," she'd suggested. "My mom has this tiny tape recorder. She got it to tape my father yelling."

"What?" I'd asked.

"My father used to yell so much when he got upset that my mom worried he might have a heart attack. So she taped him, and then afterwards, when he calmed down, she played it back to him. He hardly ever yells anymore."

I decided it was time to stop bad-mouthing Rosalie's mom—and her theories. Thanks to her, I was about to get my hands on a tape recorder.

The tape recorder was no bigger than a bar of soap. It came with a small attachable microphone. "All right then, I'll admit it," Rosalie said as she handed me the tape recorder, "sometimes—in an emergency—pranks are okay."

Truth was, lately I hadn't been thinking much about pranks. Sure, it had been fun to prank Leblanc into hiring me. But catching Leblanc in the act wasn't about teasing him or getting attention. It wasn't even about feeling angry. No, this prank was a way to right a wrong. Knowing that felt good. Better, come to think of it, than any prank had ever made me feel.

"It's going to be a late night," Leblanc said when I turned up at the dock that evening. "You and I are going out on a Zodiac. Instead of cleaning, why don't you have a nap in the clubhouse?"

Getting paid to sleep sounded like a sweet deal. Besides, I was exhausted. Though the clubhouse couch smelled musty, and there were springs sticking out at the bottom, I fell right asleep. I had a lot of dreams. Petit Fou and Rosalie were in most of them. I even dreamt about Mr. Quincy. In my dream, he was at assembly, telling students I'd drowned in the Saguenay. "He was a prankster," Mr. Quincy said, nodding his head sadly. "Only, the last prank was on him."

It was after midnight when Leblanc shook me awake. "There's a group of tourists ready to pay big bucks to go whale watching this time tomorrow. We're going on a practice run. I need a pair of young ears to listen for whales."

Leblanc let the motor idle as he pored over a map. When he put the map down, he pointed at a damp cushion in the boat's stern. As I sat down, I stuck my hands into my pockets. I felt the hard ridges of the camera and, in the other pocket, the tape recorder. I'd rigged things up so the wire that attached the microphone to the tape recorder was hidden inside the sleeve of my windbreaker. With one finger, I searched for the tape recorder's switch. I was pretty sure I'd be able to flick it on without Leblanc noticing.

At night, the waters of the Saguenay were as black as the sky. The sharp scent of pine filled my nostrils as the Zodiac took off. All I could see of Leblanc was his back, hunched over the wheel. "I got really close to a humpback the other night," he muttered, without turning around.

Gee, I thought as I flicked on the switch to the tape recorder and tugged the tiny microphone out from my sleeve and into my palm, this is going to be easier than I thought.

"Humpbacks?" I asked, leaning in toward him. "Pretty rare out here, aren't they?"

Leblanc grunted. I couldn't tell whether that meant yes or no.

"How close did you get?" I asked, careful to keep the excitement out of my voice.

"I'd say five meters, maybe four," Leblanc said, turning around to face me. Was he trying to gauge my reaction?

"Cool!" I said. My answer seemed to satisfy him.

It was hard to know exactly where we were. Out in the dark, you couldn't spot landmarks. The waters we were traveling through had narrowed. There were no beaches in this area, just scraggly shrubs that grew close to the shore. Overhead I could make out the outline of hydroelectric cables crisscrossing the sky.

If there were whales around, they were staying clear of the Zodiac. My eyes dropped to the floor of the boat. A coil of thick cord lay next to a pile of blankets. If I get cold, I thought, I could grab a blanket. Just then I saw something roll under the blankets. Was there an animal on board?

It was a good thing I didn't say anything, because a second later I spotted another piece of what looked like thick cord. Only this was dark brown—and it was moving. Which is when I realized it wasn't cord at all. It was a braid. And I only knew one person with braids.

Chapter Thirteen

Partly, I was pissed off. What was Rosalie thinking? If Leblanc found her, we'd be in hot—or more likely, cold water. But another part of me felt glad she was along for the ride.

I was trying to think of a way to signal Rosalie that I'd spotted her, when I heard a faint *whoosh*. I spun to the right. So did Leblanc, and as he did, he turned on the boat's searchlight. Its hazy beam picked up the reflection of what looked like a shiny white half moon on the water's surface. Then there were more of the half-moon shapes. They were up ahead, near a small island.

"Belugas," Leblanc whispered.

"I think it's time to take some pictures," I said, pulling out my camera. Leblanc couldn't have heard me over the sound of the motor, but I needed photographic evidence—and this was my chance. I positioned myself so I could include not just whales, but also part of the Zodiac.

When we were so close to the pod— there were six belugas in all—that I could have touched their blubbery skin, Leblanc switched off the motor. "Something's wrong with this gas gauge," he muttered. "I filled the bloody tank this afternoon."

He leaned over the instrument panel and began fiddling with the gauge. He was so intent on fixing whatever was wrong, he didn't seem to notice the belugas—or that I was taking pictures.

When one beluga dove, the cool spray left a misty film on my camera lens. Within a couple of minutes I'd shot a roll of film. Just as I was putting in another roll, Leblanc turned toward me. "I fixed the—," he announced, but then his eyes landed on my camera. "Hand that over! Now!" he shouted, coming toward me and tugging the camera from my neck.

I stepped back, tucking the roll of used film into the pocket of my life jacket. "What's wrong?" I asked, trying to keep my voice calm, though my arms and legs felt wobbly.

"You—you!" Leblanc sputtered. "I should have known you were in cahoots with Jean Racine, that useless do-gooder."

"I don't know what you're tal—," I began, but I never got to finish my sentence.

"I want you off this boat!" Leblanc barked. Then he lunged at me, picking me up by the waist and hoisting me over his shoulders. I tried to kick myself free, but it didn't work.

"I'm going to dump you on that island. Let's see how long it takes your uncle to find you!" As he shouted, the tape recorder—without the wire or the microphone, which must have come undone—dropped from my pocket, landing a few inches from the pile of blankets. I watched Rosalie's thin fingers emerge from under the blankets and grab the tape recorder.

"I've had it with you! I can't take it anymore!" a strange male voice crackled.

"I've told you before, and I'm telling you again. Cut it OUT!"

I'd never heard anyone sound so angry. Whoever it was was out of control.

"Where's that voice coming from?" Leblanc called out.

"I've had it with you! I can't take it any more!" the voice repeated, even more loudly than before. This time I noticed some static in the background, which is when I figured out who it was. Rosalie's father! Rosalie had rewound the tape and was playing it back at maximum volume.

"What's going on?" Leblanc yelled. Without knowing it, he'd loosened his grip on me. I jumped to the floor, landing near the pile of blankets. Don't move, Rosalie, I thought to myself.

There was no time for a plan, but I had to do something. Just then I noticed a slight wiggling in the cord next to the blankets. It's Rosalie, I thought. She's pulling on one end. But why? What is she trying to tell me?

Then I got it. You're brilliant, Rosalie, I thought. Absolutely brilliant. I reached for the cord and looped it around Leblanc's ankles.

"What the—?" Leblanc was still trying to figure out where the voice was coming from. As I tugged on one end of the cord, Rosalie leapt up from under the blankets and crashed into Leblanc's knees.

Leblanc fell flat on the floor, head first, making a thud as he landed.

I thought he'd try to get up, but he didn't. He just lay there, breathing heavily.

"I think we knocked him out," Rosalie said. The two of us worked quickly, wrapping the cord around Leblanc's body so he wouldn't be able to use his hands or feet.

We dragged him over to the pile of blankets. He didn't look too happy when he began to come to. "What's she doing here?" he asked, eyeing Rosalie.

"Sorry about all the yelling," Rosalie said, pulling out the tape recorder and turning it back on. "I can't take it anymore!" her father's voice blared.

"That was just my father," she added, grinning up at Leblanc. "Don't worry, he's learning to control his temper."

On the way back, I took over at the wheel. My hands tingled with excitement. Once I got us past the small island, all I'd have to do was follow the path of the Saguenay back to Tadoussac.

Rosalie sat, squatted, close to Leblanc. "Darned kids. You won't get away with this!" he muttered. A minute later, when he tried to break free, Rosalie tightened the cord around him. After a while he stopped squirming and just stared straight ahead at the water, his chest heaving up and down.

The sky was beginning to turn pinkish orange when we reached the confluence. Which was when this totally incredible thing happened. The kind of thing you might think only happens in books or movies.

We heard splashing. Then, as if a water fountain was bursting from the bottom of the Saguenay, this huge spray of water shot up into the air. It was a whale coming up for air. As its tail rose into the sky, I spotted the familiar triangular scar.

Chapter Fourteen

If you read the Tadoussac newspaper or watch the news, you'll know what happened next. Leblanc lost his boating license and had to pay a huge fine. If you ask me, he kind of liked the attention. In the newspaper photographs, he's smiling so much you'd think he was some kind of soap-opera star. And in a way, as Aunt Daisy said, he was.

Other Zodiac operators were scared by what had happened to Leblanc, so there were a lot fewer violations of the whale-watching rules that summer.

As for Rosalie and me, I guess you could say we became kind of like local heroes. We got free hot dogs and fries at the chip wagon, and the guys at Uncle Jean's kayaking company stopped giving me the crummy jobs. There were still two weeks till I had to go back to Montreal to start over at a new school—but to tell you the truth, I didn't want to leave.

I guess sometimes when you're really dreading something, it can end up surprising you. I've got to try to remember that in the future.

Rosalie and I had this routine. She'd meet me at the launching area after work. Sometimes she'd bring granola bars and we'd walk back to the B&B, stopping to sit on the rocks and look for whales.

We didn't see Petit Fou again that summer, but as Dr. Youville said, in the case of a recovering whale, no news is good news. Plus I had this strange feeling that Petit Fou was out there, keeping an eye on all of us.

"So," Rosalie wanted to know one evening as we tossed pebbles into the Saguenay and watched the water ripple, "planning any pranks?"

"No more pranks!" I told her. Only, this time I meant it.

Acknowledgments

Un grand merci to Marie-Louise Gay for her generous encouragement.

This book would not have been possible without help from the staff at the Marine Mammal Interpretation Centre in Tadoussac, and especially from naturalist Robert Michaud, research director of the Groupe de recherche et d'éducation sur les mammifères marins. I'm also grateful to Alain Dumais, biologist and kayaking guide, and to Captain Mario Tremblay of le Groupe Dufour.

Special thanks to Claire Rothman and Evadne Anderson for their valuable comments on the manuscript; to Viva Singer for letting me talk about this project nonstop and agreeing to read several versions; and to Deena Sacks, Donna Haberman, Rina Singh, Max and Celine Polak for reading the manuscript.

Thanks also to Erica Lighter, Angad Singh and Daniel Haberman for giving me a kid's point of view; to Barbara Vininsky, my most loyal supporter; and to Andrew Wooldridge of Orca Books for his faith in the project and wise guidance.

Finally, thanks to my daughter Alicia for bringing home great stories.

Titles in the Series

orca soundings